Services for Children:
An Agenda for Research

Committee on Child Development Research
and Public Policy

Assembly of Behavioral
and Social Sciences

National Research Council

NATIONAL ACADEMY PRESS
Washington, D.C. 1981

NOTICE: The project that is the subject of this report was approved by the Governing Board of the National Research Council, whose members are drawn from the Councils of the National Academy of Sciences, the National Academy of Engineering, and the Institute of Medicine. The members of the Committee responsible for the report were chosen for their special competences and with regard for appropriate balance.

This report has been reviewed by a group other than the authors according to procedures approved by a Report Review Committee consisting of members of the National Academy of Sciences, the National Academy of Engineering, and the Institute of Medicine.

The National Research Council was established by the National Academy of Sciences in 1916 to associate the broad community of science and technology with the Academy's purposes of furthering knowledge and of advising the federal government. The Council operates in accordance with general policies determined by the Academy under the authority of its congressional charter of 1863, which establishes the Academy as a private, nonprofit, self-governing membership corporation. The Council has become the principal operating agency of both the National Academy of Sciences and the National Academy of Engineering in the conduct of their services to the government, the public, and the scientific and engineering communities. It is administered jointly by both Academies and the Institute of Medicine. The National Academy of Engineering and the Institute of Medicine were established in 1964 and 1970, respectively, under the charter of the National Academy of Sciences.

Library of Congress Catalog Card Number 81-81819

International Standard Book Number 0-309-03147-8

Available from

NATIONAL ACADEMY PRESS
2101 Constitution Ave., N.W.
Washington, D.C. 20418

Printed in the United States of America

STUDY PROJECT ON

CHILDREN'S SERVICES

LAURENCE E. LYNN, JR., Chair, John F. Kennedy School
of Government, Harvard University
SARANE S. BOOCOCK, Department of Sociology, Rutgers
University
URIE BRONFENBRENNER, Department of Human Development
and Family Studies, Cornell University
LEWIS H. BUTLER, Health Policy Program, School of
Medicine, University of California, San Francisco
JOHN P. DEMOS, Department of History, Brandeis
University
ROCHEL GELMAN, Department of Psychology, University
of Pennsylvania
E. MAVIS HETHERINGTON, Department of Psychology,
University of Virginia
ROBERT B. HILL, National Urban League, Inc.,
Washington, D.C.
A. SIDNEY JOHNSON, III, Family Impact Seminar, George
Washington University
ALFRED J. KAHN, School of Social Work, Columbia
University
RICHARD J. LIGHT, Graduate School of Education,
Harvard University
ELEANOR E. MACCOBY, Department of Psychology,
Stanford University Law School, Stanford University
ROBERT H. MNOOKIN, Law School, Stanford University
RICHARD R. NELSON, Department of Economics, Yale
University

iii

iv

COMMITTEE ON

CHILD DEVELOPMENT

RESEARCH AND PUBLIC POLICY

---

v

CONTENTS

PREFACE

When the Committee on Child Development Research and
Public Policy began this project--to develop a
research agenda for children's services--the task
appeared quite manageable. We were familiar with
issues relating to the development and well-being of
children, had had experience with a variety of
federal, state, and local services for children, and
had been involved in research on children's
services. Furthermore, we felt we already had a good
understanding of the problem. Although there are
policies and programs for children at many different
levels of government, children's services lack
coherence, focus, and a sense of direction. Some
children are well-served, others are served not at
all, and still others seem to be actually harmed by
fumbling governmental efforts to assist them.
Accordingly, we welcomed the task, and agreed to

ix

consult experts, review available literature, reflect, and write what we anticipated would be a crisp and concise diagnosis and prescription for future research.

After more than two years of work, we have reached one unanimous conclusion: We would rather deliver children's services, or even raise children, than prepare a report on the subject. The task, in other words, has been anything but easy, and we were often tempted to give up in frustration. The reason was not lack of cooperation from people who knew and cared about the delivery of services to children. We have had many fruitful conversations with virtually everyone whom we sought out. Rather, the difficulty lay in our approach and in the effort to develop a convincing justification for it.

Our recommendation about how research can lead to improvement in children's services and children's lives emerged with great force from our consultation and deliberations: research on children's services, as well as the services themselves, must be more fundamentally concerned with the child and informed by an understanding of the way children live and manage. Both research and services approach children from dozens of specialized perspectives. They are hardly ever viewed as entire human beings in their homes, families, and community environments, services are hardly ever designed in the light of that kind of broad understanding of children's lives and the people and forces that shape them. Largely for this reason, services for children are falling short of the expectations of parents, program administrators, and legislators.

There seemed to be three problems in explaining and justifying this rcommendation.

First, it might sound too simplistic or obvious, the prelude to another appeal for "holistic conceptualizations" and "comprehensive policy," which is standard fare from a committee such as ours, but hardly helpful to people who actually do research, design policies, or deliver services. As one early reader put it: Is that all we can say? At times we were tempted to deliver a message that appeared to make a grander appeal: researchers should concentrate on identifying gaps in existing research--questions we are not addressing, knowledge we do not have--and large increases in expenditures are needed to finance major studies, longitudinal panels, needs assessments, better theory, etc. In the end we chose to resist this temptation. Although it is difficult to state the case for what may seem obvious, in this instance we felt the effort had to be made.

Second, research on "how children live and manage," however edifying, might go for naught as far as policy making is concerned and end up being merely more social science research gathering dust on the shelves. Congress, executive agencies, service providers, and researchers are in fact specialized, categorical, and problem-oriented. They see children in terms of specific kinds of problems, specific developmental needs, or concrete circumstances of deprivation. The policy audience has little interest in research that does not have operational applications or in ideas that cannot be implemented by the existing service system.

Thus, a more efficacious message might be that we must do more of what we are doing now but do it better, and at the same time foster innovative additions to the existing array of children's services. We believe this, and we say now: If nothing else, we must do more of what we are doing now, do it better, and foster innovation. We do not think this enough.

Third, our message may be wrong in some fundamental sense. Some of us involved in this project were also recently involved in an assessment of research needs for urban policy. Participants in that study contemplated the same kind of recommendation--focus on the city in toto rather than on specialized views of its problems. In the case of cities, however, the more organic or holistic approach was rejected. For a variety of reasons, the city did not seem to be the right unit of analysis; more specialized approaches seemed justified. Maybe the case of services for children is similar: although the object of concern, the child may be an inappropriate focus of analysis. This is a harder issue to resolve. Yet upon reflection we still do not think that numerous specialized perspectives are a sufficient basis for policy concerning children's services.

Fragmentation in the service system is inevitable, as is the tendency for political debate to focus on particular problems and issues. The fact that programs and discussions tend to be categorical leads, however, to real difficulties with the system of children's services. Children are whole human beings. Their problems and needs are connected and not always readily treated piecemeal by categories. For this reason, there are pressures to connect and unify various parts of the service system, pressures that to a certain extent counterbalance the forces leading to further specialization of the parts of the system. Because children's needs are not neatly dividable and because an important part of the ongoing policy debate involves considerations that cut across categories, it is exceedingly important that a considerable portion of research not be bound by existing categories.

In particular, we think that private foundations and other research funding agencies not preoccupied with particular programmatic responsibilities play a major role in supporting research that is not categorical, research that proceeds from a broader view of how children live and manage. This is one of our principal recommendations.

Is such a humanistic, idealistic appeal practical? Is it right? We think so, but doubts on this score are not unwarranted, and, as we have said, the case is not easy to make. Changing the world of research, policy, and services to accommodate new perspectives is never easy. You will no doubt sense this as you read what follows. We urge you to consider the message carefully; we try to give several examples of what we mean; and we suggest funding strategies that might stimulate the right kinds of change. Admittedly it is not a message that, if heeded, could better the lot of children today. Yet if taken seriously and put into practice, it can have a powerful influence tomorrow. Children will still be there.

This report represents an attempt to discover and synthesize the views of a large number of people who have extensive experience in the field of research on services for children and who are thoroughly familiar with its literature. Although we recognize that education is the most prominent and universal service provided both publicly and privately to children in our society, we have not dealt in this report with the development and implementation of curricular education programs. We have instead focused on the range of child welfare, health, juvenile justice, recreation, child development, and family support services provided to children. Views on the quality and usefulness of existing research differ widely, ranging from qualified praise to qualified condemnation, and opinions on what changes are needed are similarly wide-ranging. We listened carefully and, in the light of our own views and experiences, prepared what we believe to be a fair assessment and prescription concerning research on children's services. This is our report, however, and inescapably reflects the subjectivity with which we approach the topic. Accordingly, we have chosen not to include the copious footnotes and accounts of scientific disagreement that would be characteristic of a review of the literature or a state-of-the-art survey.

We would like to acknowledge the support and encouragement of Terry Saario and the Ford Foundation in the launching and completion of this report. She had the vision that an effort of this kind was needed, shared our frustrations in searching for a proper approach to the subject, and urged us to present our conclusions as crisply and forcefully as possible.

The study project was undertaken by the members of the Committee on Child Development Research and Public Policy in 1978. Although the membership of the committee changed in the course of the project, those who made the original commitment persevered. By bringing diverse perspectives to bear on the subject, they ultimately helped ensure that the effort was co-opted by no particular perspective but instead was preoccupied with formulating a message aimed at helping children. Special thanks are due Sheldon H. White, ex officio member of the committee, whose ideas inspire the report at many points, especially in the first chapter.

Study director for the project was Cheryl D. Hayes, who organized and directed a substantial consultation effort as well as the drafting of this report. She was assisted by Wendy A. Warring, who served as research assistant, and by Jeffrey R. Travers, who provided useful criticisms of early drafts. Frank Farrow also assisted in the drafting process.

The committee would also like to thank David A. Goslin, executive director of the Assembly of Behavioral and Social Sciences, for his advice and assistance at many points during the project, and Christine L. McShane, the Assembly editor, for her work on the report. Finally, we owe thanks to the many people, too numerous to list, who gave generously of their time and knowledge. Though absolved of responsibility for what we have produced, they provided the advice and assistance that made it possible to say anything at all.

LAURENCE E. LYNN, JR.
Chair, Study Project on Children's Services

Services for
Children:
An Agenda for Research

HISTORICAL
BACKGROUND

Since American colonists began binding orphaned and
abandoned youth in craft apprenticeships, people and
organizations outside the family have shared
responsibility for the care and well-being of
children. The role of these institutions--schools,
asylums, welfare agencies, courts, churches and
charities, and foster homes--has steadily expanded in
response to specific problems and needs. This
expansion has always been accompanied by
controversy. What do children need that parents
cannot provide or cannot provide without help? When
should government rather than private and charitable
groups be involved in addressing those needs? Is
public assistance to and protection of children a
federal, state, or local responsibility? Should
publicly supported services for children be available
to all children "at risk" or only to the poor?

1

In recent decades, as the growth in public programs that benefit children has accelerated, such questions have become more insistent, and controversies among elected officials, practitioners, and parents concerning public policies affecting children have become even more intense and widespread (Kenniston and the Carnegie Council on Children 1978, Sheehan 1977, Case Western Reserve University 1977, Steiner 1976, National Research Council 1976). Because these issues are both value-laden and political, they will not be "resolved" by research alone. Unless future research on children's services takes fundamentally new directions, however, the available knowledge, information, and ideas will be insufficient to provide the foundations for wise political choices on public policies and programs affecting children. Basic issues will remain unaddressed, and shortcomings in the existing system of services to children—unmet and poorly met needs, public efforts that seem to conflict with each other or to undermine private efforts—will become more severe and prove increasingly harmful to the interests of children and their families.

The purpose of this report is to chart some of the new directions that research on children's services should take and to underscore the importance of this research to future policy debates concerning children's services. In particular, we shall urge that a significant body of research should focus on children, rather than on specific agencies or programs, as the subject of study.

Public
Programs for
Children

"Children's services" comprise numerous activities designed to meet children's physical, social, emotional, and educational needs. One survey of federal expenditures for children, conducted in 1976, identified some 260 programs that provide services to children and their families as their major function (Rose 1976). The numerous public programs for children from birth to 18 years of age can be grouped by their general functions into seven categories, which are described below.

Child welfare services are generally provided by public and private agencies and proprietary agencies to ensure continuation or replacement of parental care; examples are foster care, adoption services, and protective services. Day care, once generally considered part of this category of services, has more recently been grouped with child development and early childhood education services, unless it is provided for therapeutic or protective purposes. Child welfare services may involve the placement of a child outside his or her family in adoptive, foster care, or institutional settings; they may also involve support, counseling, or strengthening a family to keep it intact as well as programs for treatment and socialization.

Child development and early childhood education services generally include day care for infants and children, prekindergarten, nursery schools, and other services designed to maximize the physical, emotional, and cognitive development of the young child. Project Head Start in the Office of Human Development Services of the Department of Health, Education, and Welfare (now the U.S. Department of Health and Human Services and the U.S. Department of Education) has become a prototype for compensatory early childhood education programs intended to increase the overall competence of economically disadvantaged preschool children.

Education services include programs designed to meet the needs for special education of particular groups of children. In addition to standard educational programs and supportive services (such as transportation) for the handicapped, vocational education, and education for children who do not speak English, these programs provide special services to educationally deprived or disadvantaged children, neglected or delinquent children in institutions, Indian children, and gifted and talented children.

Child health and mental health services include

primary care for children and prenatal care for mothers. These services typically involve screening, diagnosis, treatment, and follow-up of physical and mental illness. This category also includes nutrition and feeding programs. Recipients of services may receive care on an out-patient basis or within institutional settings such as hospitals.

Youth services include activities that focus on the special needs of youths other than those generally addressed by health and education programs. They include programs for recreation, the prevention and treatment of drug and alcohol abuse, pregnancy prevention and abortion, employment training, and individual and group counseling. Services may be provided in residential settings, but they are typically delivered through daytime community-based programs.

Juvenile justice services include the range of services provided in conjunction with or as a substitute for the activities of the police and the juvenile courts. This category incorporates the more traditional functions of probation and detention as well as the placement and care of runaways and abused and neglected children for whom training schools and residential correctional facilities are usually inappropriate. States vary widely in their definitions of juvenile justice services. In some instances these services are provided by child welfare agencies; in others they are provided by adult correctional or juvenile justice agencies.

Other statutory and publicly supported social services that affect children include a variety of supportive services, usually in conjunction with cash assistance programs, such as special counseling, referral and outreach, vacations, budgeting, and educational programs.

These categories are not mutually exclusive. Programs may overlap categories or might as easily be placed in one category as another. In many instances, for example, juvenile justice and youth services are interchangeable labels for the same program. Alcohol and drug abuse programs are often classified as both youth and health services. Nevertheless, such a typology is useful because it reflects the terms and categories that policy makers typically use.

The existing structure of children's services reflects the gradual assumption of responsibility for particular problems and categories of children by all levels of government throughout the nation's history. Because of the nature of the political process, services have been created and expanded in an incremental, piecemeal way. They are not the manifestation of a comprehensive and clearly rationalized national policy to coordinate public and private efforts on behalf of children. Rather, they comprise numerous separately conceived and administered parts, reflecting an exceedingly large and diverse number of independent actions by all levels and branches of government (Lynn 1978).

Throughout American history, local governments and private charities protected and cared for children who were homeless, abandoned, or neglected. Colonial courts placed these children in substitute families as servants and apprentices; later, with the advent of orphanages and asylums, children without families were cared for in institutions. In the 19th century the states began to provide education, child welfare services, and some public health services, a trend that accelerated in the 20th century as advocacy on behalf of children became better organized and more effective. The White House Conference on the Care of Dependent Children in 1909 and the establishment of the Children's Bureau in the Department of Labor in 1912 made children's services a matter of federal interest and sparked the Mother's Pension Movement of the 1920s and ultimately the creation of the Aid to Dependent Children Program in 1935. The Children's Bureau, established as a research and information center to generate knowledge about the conditions of children's lives and plans for programs of action, institutionalized federal interest and involvement in promoting the health and well-being of children (Eliot 1962).

The Sheppard-Towner Act, passed in 1921, expanded the federal role from a responsibility for a relatively small number of children dependent on the

state to health care for pregnant women and infants.
The act aimed to reduce infant and maternal mortality
by providing the states with matching federal funds
to establish health centers for pregnant women and
infants. Although Sheppard-Towner was short-lived,
it laid important groundwork for the major federal
health care initiative in the Social Security Act of
1935. The act established the principle of social
insurance as protection against income loss due to
unemployment, old age, disability, or death. It also
provided public assistance to the poor with the Aid
to Dependent Children Program, which provided federal
grants-in-aid to the states to administer programs of
cash support and services to children in families
headed by women. The act also included provisions
for child welfare services, handicapped children's
services, and maternal and child health services.

Until the mid-1960s the federal role in providing
for children's services was limited to the programs
initiated under the Social Security Act and other
isolated initiatives, such as the School Lunch
Program. Since then, a large number of additional
federal programs have been created. Many of these
were implemented by state and local governments and
neighborhood groups; others were operated directly by
federal agencies. Lyndon Johnson's war on poverty,
drawing on research demonstrating the importance of
the first years of life in human development,
established numerous programs to enhance the

development of economically and culturally deprived young children. Most important among these was compensatory education for poor preschool children (i.e., Head Start). After Head Start, a variety of programs were established to improve children's home life (i.e., Home Start), to ensure that they received adequate diets and health care (i.e., the Special Supplemental Food Program for Women, Infants and Children and the Early and Periodic Screening, Diagnosis and Treatment Program), and to ensure an adequate public education to disadvantaged children (i.e., the Elementary and Secondary Education Act). Statutory and publicly financed children's services at both the federal and state levels continued to expand in the 1970s.

Thus, in the past several decades a complex system of statutory and publicly financed services has developed to meet the special needs of children. For families that are incompetent, ailing, or unavailable, orphan asylums, foster care, and adoption services were established to try to provide something like a home for every child. To provide an instructive and pleasant environment for small children in urban settings and to provide relief for parents under stress, preschools and day care centers were opened. Common schools arose as places to give publicly supported education to children in diverse places and stations in American society; in a wave of state enactments from about 1880 to 1937, these common schools became universal and compulsory. With all children required to attend school and with public expectations that such schooling would be egalitarian and optimal for all children, subsequent school-related activities were committed to providing support to handicapped children, bilingual or bicultural children, children with emotional problems, and educationally gifted children. For youths who were increasingly being displaced from jobs, in a prolongation of what has been called social adolescence, social facilities offered recreational programs, employment training and counseling, services for unmarried mothers, and, more recently, treatment for drug and alcohol abuse and pregnancy prevention and abortion. With neither families nor schools perfectly attuned to the problems of a prolonged adolescence, with the loss of community control mechanisms as more families settled in urban environments, and with the growth in the number of immigrant families, courts took on the functions of youth control and discipline through the concept of status offenses. A variety of auxiliary mechanisms arose in conjunction with such court activities, ranging from auxiliary diagnostic and counseling facilities to the establishment of reformatories and training schools.

As these hundreds of programs have come into existence, they have become the seeds for further progammatic and professional evolution. These seeds,

at first widely scattered among states and
localities, have multiplied and become more dense.
The density itself becomes a problem. Seeds-of-a-
kind, such as local child welfare services or state
institutions, produce new structures to cope with
these problems, such as local, state, or federal
coordinating and regulatory agencies. Service
providers form professional associations and national
organizations for comunication, regulation, and
advocacy. The resulting growth is profuse, richly
varied, and tangled.

Services are highly diverse in nature and include
medical care, foster care, day care, remedial
instruction, recreation, nutrition, supervision and
counseling. Some are provided by highly trained
professionals, such as physicians, psychologists,
social workers, and teachers; others are provided by
paraprofessionals, volunteers, and parents. Some
services, such as health care and education, are
provided directly to children; others, such as
homemaker services and public assistance, benefit
children indirectly as members of a family or
household. Some services are directed to poor
children and their families, while others, such as
subsidized school lunches and milk, are available to
virtually all children. Still other services are
intended to meet the special needs of certain
children without regard for ability to pay, such as
shelters for runaway youths, programs for the

prevention of drug and alcohol abuse, and special education programs for the physically and mentally handicapped. For the most part, programs provide for specific treatments or interventions to help alleviate specific problems. The problem of child abuse, for example, or the problem of infant mortality, or the problem of teenage drug abuse all have identifiable symptoms. Public programs are designed to treat those symptoms by removing a child from an abusive parent, providing prenatal care to pregnant mothers who are at high risk, or teaching adolescents about the harmful effects of narcotics use.

Large amounts of public resources are now being provided for children participating in a variety of federal, state, and local programs. In 1935, child welfare services provided under the Social Security Act received approximately $1.5 million of federal funds in grants-in-aid to the states; in 1977 more than $1 billion in federal funds was allocated to these services under Title XX of the Social Security Act alone (U.S. Office of Management and Budget 1977). This public financing of services for children is, for the most part, for quite specific purposes. Grants for categorical programs specify in detail eligibility requirements and the nature of the services to be provided. In order to obtain funds, public and private agencies tend to label children according to the characteristics specified for

program eligibility. If, for example, funds are
available for mentally retarded children, children
who are legally identified as wards of the state, or
"predelinquent" children, agencies tend to identify
the needs of children in these terms.

Financial and administrative arrangements vary.
Some services are financed and delivered by churches
or other private charitable groups. Many are
financed and operated by public agencies of the
states or municipalities. Others are administered by
the states with substantial federal financial
contributions through revenue sharing or block
grants, which provide fiscal support without
specifying its use. Many more, although delivered by
state and local agencies or private organizations,
are financed and regulated by the federal government
through categorical grants that provide funds for
designated purposes. With the increase in the
availability of federal grants, private, voluntary
child welfare agencies, which have retained primary
responsibility for service delivery, have become
increasingly dependent on federal support.

Program authority is widely dispersed among all
levels of government. Twenty-two separate federal
agencies in five cabinet-level departments are
authorized to support children's programs (Hayes and
Davis 1979). At the state level still other agencies
may be involved. In Illinois, for example, a state
with a relatively long public welfare tradition, at

least 11 state agencies are responsible for serving children. A child may receive special tutoring for a learning disability at school. If a child is too young for school and has a mother who works, he or she may be cared for at a publicly subsidized day care center. A child may receive health check-ups and innoculations at a "well child" clinic, but if he or she is sick, the child must see a private physician, whose fee will be paid by the Illinois welfare department. If she or he has some physical or mental handicap, services are likely to be provided in still another location. If the child is under age four and the family is unable to provide an adequate diet, he or she may be taken to yet another health clinic to receive yet another check-up in order to be eligible to receive supplemental food.

Children in need have unquestionably benefited from these public efforts on their behalf. At the same time, our perceptions of children's needs are increasingly distorted by the necessity of viewing them through a categorical service structure that may be unmanageably complex, expensive, and confusing. In the process of program creation, little thought was given to how these separate programs might be coordinated or might reinforce one another, the extent to which their administrative procedures may duplicate or be at cross purposes with one another, the likelihood of unintended consequences, or the extent to which these programs may not adequately

meet children's health and nutrition requirements.
The resulting symptoms of dysfunction are of various
kinds.

First, existing services do not necessarily
address all or even the most important needs of
individual children. It is not unusual for a child
with several problems (a troubled adolescent, for
example) to receive a label from an available program
(drug abuser or delinquent, for example) when, in
fact, his or her troubles do not fall into one
prescribed category--or into a prescribed category at
all. A child may run away from home, perform poorly
in school, have social and emotional difficulties
dealing with peers, and use drugs and alcohol.
Perhaps, in addition, he or she may have encounters
with the police and/or juvenile authorities. Chances
are that when and if this child is brought into the
service system he or she will be diagnosed and
treated for only one type of problem--perhaps a
learning difficulty, a mental health disorder, or on
a juvenile delinquency charge. If the treatment
corresponding to the diagnosis is unsuccessful, he or
she may be referred for another service or shuttled
between programs and agencies. The child will
probably not, however, receive help that coordinates
attention to the various problems simultaneously.

Second, services do not reach all the children who
need them or are eligible to receive them. In the
first nine years of the Early and Periodic Screening,

Diagnosis and Treatment Program (EPSDT), for example, fewer than one-quarter of the eligible children were screened. Moreover, only about 50 percent of those who were screened and found to need treatment ever received it. Similarly, Head Start and the bilingual education programs have reached only a small number of the children who are eligible and would benefit from them (Children's Defense Fund 1977, Steiner 1976).

Third, various institutions administering children's programs rarely communicate with one another, largely because they operate on different premises, with different professional orientations, and different arrangements of governance. Because there is no central point of coordination in the system, agencies frequently duplicate or overlap administrative and/or service functions, while others are not performed at all. In Massachusetts, for example, several agencies perform diagnostic tests as part of their in-take procedures. Although these tests may focus on slightly different aspects of physical, psychological, or cognitive development, there is substantial duplication among them. A child served by more than one agency or enrolled in more than one program thus may be tested several times (Sheehan 1977). And the agencies often are unable to demonstrate that their tests are uniquely related to their services or that knowledge of the results of required testing increases the effectiveness of their services.

In California, several agencies have general responsibility for children who are mentally retarded and mentally disturbed, yet there is no clear statutory responsibility for those who are severely mentally impaired.[1] The closing of many state-operated residential care facilities, which formerly housed these children, has placed the burden of their care on one or another local agency and on their families. In many communities, however, as programs have developed to educate the mentally retarded and to treat the mentally disturbed, the special needs of children who are severely mentally impaired have been overlooked.

Fourth, services frequently have harmful negative effects that are unintended and that may outweigh their benefits to a child's development. Efforts to eliminate these unwanted effects often introduce additional complexity into the services system. "Juvenile delinquency," for example, was a label devised to keep children out of the adult criminal justice system in order to protect them from the stigma associated with being prosecuted as adults and to prevent their being socialized into a life of

---

[1]The term mentally retarded refers to a condition of deficient intellectual and perceptual abilities. The term mentally disturbed refers to a condition of emotional or psychological illness or malfunction apart from retardation. Mentally impaired is a generic term for both types of mental malfunction, which may be acute or chronic.

crime through incarceration with adult criminals. However, the effect of employing this label, regardless of the seriousness of the offense, was to create another classification—juvenile delinquent— that stigmatized children who committed relatively minor offenses. Thus, still another label—status offender—was devised to classify children, such as runaways and truants, whose actions were judged to be offenses only because of their age and would not be so judged if committed by adults.

Finally, because services are oriented toward the treatment of problems, there is little impetus to develop preventive services or services that support or reinforce children's strengths or healthy personal development. Indeed, local programs to assist gifted children or to encourage the development of a child's natural advantages may be viewed by public authorities as at odds or in competition with attempts to eliminate the invidious consequences of disadvantage or deprivation.

The above diagnosis does not imply that we believe that decision making and the administration of children's services should be heavily centralized. Many of us strongly believe that certain parts of the system are badly in need of some integration, but integration in general would not be a cure for all ills. The pluralistic nature of American politics and the requirement for a certain narrow coherence in the administration of programs impose real constraints on the extent of feasible centralization. A decentralized, pluralistic system displays a certain flexibility, creativity, and vigor. We call attention, however, to the fact that a decentralized, pluralistic system of child services has certain innate problems. Research relevant to these problems is badly needed.

Research on
Children's
Services

One can find scattered research activities among the seed service programs and institutions that were scattered throughout the country prior to 1890. The many local institutions provided the beginnings of local social statistics and demography, supplying rudimentary needs assessments for their regions and offering data relevant to their own accountability; written descriptions of programs were often available. More or less evidential arguments dealt with the essential characteristics of children and families served by these seed programs. Some of this information inevitably was biased, and there began the practice, prevalent for years to come, of having providers of services serve as researchers and advocates for their services in public discussion. Research opened the doors to service.

From 1890 to 1960, research on children and child development became an explicit, institutionalized activity. G. Stanley Hall's Child Study Movement, which began in 1890, was clearly a smorgasbord--a variety of academic research ventures from many disciplines, a bit of philosophizing, and many odd studies and evidential arguments dealing with the various service settings and service issues that existed in American society at that time. From this pool of interests in children several distinct strains of research activity emerged. One of these was an academic strain, centering on either normative or theoretically guided studies of children's cognitive and social development. Other separate strains of research-and-service appeared as the fields of teaching, social work, pediatrics, and early education developed their own professional structures, journals, and research traditions. These several research lines became interactive--methods and ideas diffused among them--but as a consequence clusters of research journals developed, each belonging to a distinct professional specialty, and differentiations evolved in the activities of government, universities, and foundations designed to respect these professional differentiations.

With some time-outs for two wars and a major

depression, this period was one of significant growth in both the quality and quantity of services for children. The research establishments in this period acted intramurally to support the growth of information and self-reflection for the professions. From 1912 until the depression, the Children's Bureau served as a fact-finding agency, collecting statistics and case records of children with special health conditions and dependent and orphaned children. This research was put to use extramurally in the service of advocacy. During this period the service structures continued to collect the evidence and arguments relevant to the services they provided. Research supported professionalization and service expansion.

About 1960 several changes began to appear in the relationship of research to services. Prior to 1960, research was either benign or irrelevant to the service programs and institutions. Within the service establishments, professionals used data to clarify or upgrade their activities, ignoring whatever was not useful. As advocates, professionals used data selectively to justify claims for efficacy and demand. It was the task of the Congress, presumably, to referee the competing claims.

In the 1960s program planning and budgeting offices began to be attached to federal agencies, the Office of Management and Budget, and Congress. Staffed by competent researchers, they mounted an increasingly vehement critique on the evidential claims of service providers. "Policy research," inside and outside of government, produced more and more evaluations and analyses that were designed to be objective but frequently were inhibitory to the expansion of services for children. Research became double-edged.

To a significant extent, academic research and researchers were caught up in the new critical and analytic mode of the 1960s. It was initially hoped by some in academia and government that basic research on child development would provide guidance for government--would, at the least, help referee the options for investment in various kinds of service. However, basic research does not relate to federal programmatic structures as relevant units of analysis in studying children (e.g., research on cognitive development does not focus on children's needs and circumstances in the same terms as those of Title I of the Elementary and Secondary Education Act). This was perceived as a failure of basic research and it was one factor in both government disinvestment in grants in favor of contracted research and some internal self-reflection and self-criticism within academia, which led toward the growth of research on children in natural environments and in service settings. The role and utility of research was reassessed.

A great wave of task forces, commissions, and

committees came into being in the 1960s, involving mixed groups of professionals and academics and missions ranging in scope from the design of special programs for children to the effort to formulate a coherent, synthetic national policy for children. Some valiant efforts were made to set forth a coordinated national policy, notably by the Joint Commission for the Mental Health of Children (1970) in the late 1960s and by the Carnegie Council on Children in the 1970s (Kenniston and the Carnegie Council on Children 1978).

What these efforts revealed is that even heroic analytic efforts will not untangle the complexity of children's services. The tangle arose from a historic accretion of assorted programs, and will not be unraveled by principles alone. The "children's cause" remains today as Gilbert Steiner has described it--diverse professionals locked together in a love-hate relationship, partly cooperative and interfacilitating, partly redundant, partly rivalrous. Together they form a coalition able to agree on little more than the goals of advocacy-- provided one does not ask individuals to describe too carefully what they want to advocate--a diffuse, noisy, and frequently self-cancelling coalition (Steiner 1976).

In the meantime, most current research on children's services reflected the characteristics of the existing service system. Studies tended to focus on specific programs and policies; many examine the agencies and professional service providers who deliver services to children or evaluate the effectiveness of those services. The major reason for this pattern of research is that the federal government, which administers the bulk of service programs, is also by far the largest supporter of research on children's services. Federal expenditures for research and development on children's services reached approximately $94.8 million in fiscal 1977.[2] (The next-largest supporters of these activities are private foundations, which spent only an estimated $6.9 million in 1977.[3])

Federal support for research on children's services is derived from (National Research Council 1978): (1) research and development (R&D) funds associated with particular federal categorical

[2]This amount does not include large social programs, such as Head Start and the Community Mental Health Centers, which are carried on the federal budget as demonstrations, despite their substantially service-oriented objectives.

[3]Estimates of federal expenditures represent rough calculations based on unpublished data compiled for the Administration on Children, Youth and Families by the Social Research Group of the George Washington University; estimates of expenditures by private foundations were derived from compilations by the Committee staff.

programs (e.g., throughout the Department of
Education and in the Administration for Children,
Youth, and Families); (2) agencies whose primary
mission is to support social, behavioral, and
related research (e.g., the National Institute of
Mental Health); (3) statistical agencies (e.g., the
Bureau of the Census and the Bureau of Labor
Statistics); and (4) policy-making offices having
advisory and oversight responsibility for a number
of human service programs and nonprogrammatic
policies (e.g., the Office of the Assistant
Secretary for Planning and Evaluation in the
Department of Health and Human Services).

The types of research sponsored vary from agency
to agency.[4] R&D funds associated with categorical

[4]Research on children's services is of several
types: (1) Basic research is directed toward the
increase of knowledge, the improvement of
understanding, and the discovery of fundamental
relationships involved in the provision of
services. This type of research is not necessarily
applicable to the solution of immediate social
problems. (2) Applied research is aimed at showing
how existing knowledge can be used in new and
useful ways to solve immediate or anticipated
policy problems. (3) Evaluation research is
intended to determine the overall effectiveness of
programs, projects, models, strategies, materials,
methods, and costs. (4) Data collection and
analysis are related to social accounting. (5)
Demonstrations are intended to test or promote
particular methods of operation in the delivery of
services. (6) Research utilization is associated

programs tend to be used for evaluations of service delivery at the state and local levels, for demonstration and pilot projects to develop and promote improved means of providing services, or for curriculum development. R&D agencies and policy-making offices tend to support general theoretical and empirical studies of children's services. Statistical agencies are mainly supporters of data collection and special analyses of demographic data on clients and providers.

The funds associated with categorical programs support the largest amount of federal R&D on children's services--approximately 80 percent. Most of this research is on special and alternative education programs in the Office of Education. R&D agencies support approximately 19 percent of total federal R&D. The remaining 1 percent is almost equally divided between statistical agencies and policy-making offices.

The states also sponsor research on children's services. States generally support studies relating to short-term political or administrative problems, which tend to be associated with categorical programs. Total state R&D expenditures cannot be estimated from available data. State-

---

with the dissemination and diffusion of research findings, such as information systems, conferences, and publications (National Research Council 1978).

supported research generally involves monitoring program implementation and compliance because state agencies must be able to prove accountability to state legislatures, federal program authorities, and courts. Research is usually conducted under the auspices of a blue-ribbon panel or task force, which issues reports commissioned by the governor or legislature. Other state-supported research activities include: data collection and analyses of state service providers; evaluations of service programs for children that are mandated by federal or state laws and operated by the states and localities; demonstrations to develop and promote improved means of service delivery; and materials development.

Many analyses of categorical programs sponsored by government agencies are intended to highlight inequities and inefficiencies in program management and to aid decision makers in remedying unequal distributions of resources and improving the quality and uniformity of services across jurisdictions and client groups. Two examples are studies of educational services for poor and minority children and of health and child welfare services. Such research has generally compared expenditures per child with effectiveness per dollar spent in several localities within states in order to determine if expenditures and services are equitably distributed and utilized across jurisdictions and among client groups--most notably the economically disadvantaged, the handicapped, and the non-English-speaking (Kirst et al. 1980). For the most part, these analyses have been focused on individual programs and have relied on quite specific concepts of costs and effectiveness.

Private foundations sponsor a relatively small amount of research on children's services. Approximately $7.0 million was spent in fiscal 1977 by the 11 foundations with the greatest interest in research on children's services.[5] In contrast to government agencies, foundations tend to invest in discrete projects that present innovative conceptualizations, analyses of emerging trends, or problems that have yet to reach the attention of policy makers. Many foundations support demonstrations and innovative or experimental projects in service delivery to children that are of either national or local interest.

In addition, foundations tend to provide core support for private think tanks. Funds are frequently provided with the expectation that these organizations will also have other sources of support. Foundations are also a major source of support for child-advocacy activities, many of

---

[5]This figure reflects an estimate based on staff calculations.

which contain research and development components. Regardless of the source of support, studies rarely extend beyond the scope of a single program because the incentives of mission-oriented funding agencies discourage broad-gauged approaches. And because decisions affecting the design and delivery of services are made on a program-by-program basis, research tends to be oriented to the information needs of program decision makers and is generally limited in its applicability to other issues. Research supported by Title XX of the Social Security Act, for example, is unlikely to explore children's nutritional problems, even though such problems may indirectly influence the effectiveness of child care, homemaker services, and protective services supported under Title XX. Descriptive data collected by federal, state, and local agencies and private organizations for management uses are frequently not comparable. The underlying definitions of services or the characteristics of an eligible client population often differ across political jurisdictions. Availability of information concerning the circumstances of children--indicators of health, education attainment, and the like--are not consistent across states and localities; hence meaningful national aggregates are hard to come by. Similarly, data relevant to children's services collected by social science researchers, although often highly informative, have also tended to be

restricted in applicability and lacking in
comparability.

Recent advances in knowledge about the development
of children have not been fully integrated into
assessments of children's needs or the design of
services. Basic research findings have too seldom
been incorporated into categorical program studies.
For example, outcome measures for early childhood
education programs are usually based on IQ tests or
related instruments, which do not reflect current
thinking on the sequential and interactive nature of
cognitive development and which totally ignore the
dimensions of social and personality development that
have been examined in many basic research studies.

Applied research rarely influences the directions
of basic research. For example, by studying how a
wide variety of programs affect children, we should
gain insights into how the environment shapes
development. At a macro level, the key question
would be: How does provision of a given service by a
particular federal agency affect supply and demand
for this and related services by other federal
agencies, states and localities, and formal and
informal private institutions and organizations? At
a micro level, key questions are: How do the
children and their families experience the total
service system--as fragmented, confusing, and hostile
or as unified, rational, and supportive? How does
the total service system affect a child's growth and
development? Both macro and micro questions have

implications for basic understanding of organizations and people as well as for more effective service delivery. So long as research remains fragmented along programmatic lines, it is unlikely that the larger picture will be sought.

The kinds of studies conducted within the existing program framework can be judged fully appropriate only if one is content with existing programs. Studies that attempt to achieve broader perspectives concerning children's needs or the relationships between public programs and other activities--for example, supports for children provided by families, employers, and community organizations--are seldom undertaken on any significant scale. Few investigators will be pushed to seek more than partial perspectives on either children or the services they receive. An extensive search of the major journals in the fields of human resorces and social services recently conducted by Michael Kirst at Stanford University revealed no comprehensive or systematic study of children's services (Kirst et al. 1980).

A New

Direction

Often, recitations of this kind do little more than complain about the apparent impossibility of achieving comprehensive, well-coordinated, and adequately financed policies through the political process. That is not our intent. Current policies and programs reflect a constitutional system that provides for the separation of powers, administration in accordance with law, and judicial review--the collective effect of which is to encourage the formation and interplay of interest groups. There is no point in recommending policies and approaches that could only be accomplished by a central planning ministry in a single-party state.

On the other hand, we should not conclude that we are inextricably bound to exactly what exists now. The existing service structure, built by adding but not subtracting, has embedded in it governmental responses to the trends and alarms of the past. We are reluctant to add to it, because it is very complex, expensive, and confusing. But an arterio-sclerotic service structure is not responding to the trends and alarms of the present. Family structure is changing, and services--day care, schools, child welfare services--need to change to provide new cooperative arrangements with families. The trend toward a diminishing supply of jobs and prolonged adolescence implies needs for new kinds and dimensions of youth services. The deinstitutional-ization movement has generated a variety of new and tentative community-based arrangments. Demographic and monetary trends--decreasing fertility, inflationary pressure on the service sector--require reconsideration of the most efficacious means of implementing services for children.

Redesigning existing programs can improve coordination. Creating new programs or combining or modifying existing ones can improve their relevance to children's needs. Altogether new approaches can be attempted. Changes of these three kinds-- redesign, redirection, and reform--ultimately depend on convincing legislators, public administrators, and professional service providers that change can actually lead to greater benefits for children that are at the same time affordable. They are likely to come around to such beliefs, however, only if the appropriate kind of knowledge and information are available. Producing knowledge that will enhance the prospects for beneficial change is a function of research--but it must be of a broader character than the research that is prevalent now.

The contemporary structure of services for children is complex and needful of serious study if it is ever to be understood and managed. That seems to be the purpose of children's budgets (accountings of public spending for children's services and related activities) that are now being developed at several levels of government, as well as children's puzzles (studies of the tangle of local publicly supported activities intended to benefit children).

They are efforts to trace the flow of funds and authorizations as they go through the pipelines. One approach to such study would be simply to establish the structure of the current system, in order to think about more desirable alternatives and possible pathways of change. One must examine and understand knots to untie them. Another approach would be to consider how the definition of needs, policy decisions, and management might reasonably be sited at local, scate, and federal levels. Suppose some old knots can be untied--where would we want to tie new ones?

We are still uneasy and unsure about how the complex programmatic structure that exists fits constructively into children's lives--to what extent it is overloading some children (as when they are periodically pulled from their classroom for an entire day, now going to their 94-142 remedial reading program, now going to their Title I facility) and missing others completely. All the perspectives now available on children and families are episodic and limited: behavioral researchers have been looking at children in their laboratories; service providers have been looking at children from the doors of their service establishments. We need to look beyond those doors to see children in the midst of service. We need to look outside the service establishment to see how children and families spend their days and, in light of such studies, to consider how services from various sources contribute to their well-being. Thus we could illuminate the unintended consequences, both positive and negative, of service programs.

A BROADER
FRAME OF
REFERENCE

We believe there is a need for research that views
the existing system of statutory and publicly
financed programs in the context of all the sources
of support and assistance for children and their
families.

Government programs in fact account for only a
small part of the overall commitment of resources to
the care and development of children. The family is
the basic provider. Outside the family, several
"systems," ranging from the highly structured and
formal to the personal and informal, serve children
and aid parents in their child-rearing roles. Public
programs are the most formal of these systems. Other
systems include the marketplace and kin and community
networks (Bronfenbrenner 1979). Children usually
receive aid and support from more than one of these
systems. The extent to which families rely on these

systems depends on their needs, the availability of services, and their access to the services available. Patterns of use vary. Low-income families, for example, are less likely to rely on the marketplace; families with no employed workers are unlikely to receive benefits in the workplace; and families that have recently moved into a community are unlikely to depend on their neighbors for help. In addition, patterns of service use may change over time as conditions within the immediate and larger societal settings change. The increased availability of a subsidized public service, for example, may cause family members to rely less on one another. Public programs can complement, reinforce, or improve the functioning of these other, less formal systems, or they can disrupt and undermine them. To the extent that decision makers are ignorant of the interrelationships among these several systems, the latter is more likely to occur.

Research based on a broad concept of children's services would be concerned with understanding how the circumstances in which families live and manage affect children's development and how these circumstances can be altered to promote growth and socialization or to deal with more specific problems. Such studies would examine how children's needs develop in different contexts, how service responses are initiated, with what effects on

children, families, and society. Different racial,
ethnic, social, or economic subgroups could be
compared in these terms. Cross-national transfer of
data and findings would add an important dimension to
the study of children's services.[6] A broader
approach would encourage consideration of how the
adoption of public policies and practices can improve
the overall circumstances in which children live and
develop.

[6]While we did not conduct an extensive survey of
international studies of services for children,
several useful illustrations come to mind. A British
longitudinal study, in which a birth cohort has been
studied and followed since 1958, has yielded findings
relevant to child development and a variety of
service issues (Davies et al. 1972, Fogelman 1976).
A multivolume series on child care was produced by an
International Study Group for Child Care (Robinson
and Robinson 1972-1979). Werner (1979) summarized
available knowledge about the physical, cognitive,
and social development of chidren living in the
developing countries of Africa, Asia, Latin America,
and Oceana, which are experiencing rapid social
change. Rapoport and Rapoport and their
collaborators (1977) have summarized American and
British literature on emerging patterns of parenting
and their known effects. Kamerman and Kahn (1981)
have studied the known rationales, consequences, and
costs of alternative service and benefit packages in
six countries with different policy approaches to
families in which parents of infants and toddlers
work. Bradshaw and Piachaud (1980) have compared the
systems of child support and the economic value of
that support in European countries.

In this chapter we try to show by three examples how enlarging the frame of reference for studying children's services changes the focus of research questions and shifts the terms of policy debate. These include: child care, services for youth development, and the costs and benefits of financing children's services.

Child
Care

In America today more mothers than ever before are working outside the home: 59 percent of those with school-age children and 43 percent of those with children not yet of school age (U.S. Department of Labor 1980). More than half of all children under the age of 18 live in families in which the mother works or is looking for work, compared with only 39 percent in 1970 (U.S. Department of Labor 1980).

There has been a substantial increase in the proportion of families with only one parent present. Although most children continue to live with two parents, almost one of every five children under the age of 18 is living with a single parent—a rate that is more than 40 percent higher than that in 1970 (U.S. Department of Labor 1980). This increase has been most rapid among families with children under age 6. The vast majority of single-parent families

are headed by mothers; only a small proportion
(approximately 1.5 percent) are headed by fathers
(U.S. Department of Labor 1980).

Comparative employment rates for women with
children show a substantially higher proportion of
single-parent mothers in the labor force (although
the greatest increase has been among mothers in
two-parent families). In 1979, nearly 72 percent of
single-parent mothers with children ages 6-17 and 56
percent of those with children under 6 were employed
or looking for work; nearly 84 percent of those who
worked were working full time. In the same year, 59
percent of mothers in two-parent families with
children of school age and 43 percent of those with
preschool-age children were in the labor force; 66
percent of them were working full time (U.S.
Department of Labor 1980).

In sum, as the number of single-parent families
increases and as the number of mothers in single-
parent and two-parent families seeking outside
employment increases, fewer adults remain at home to
care for children. What are the implications of
these trends? What does it mean that more mothers,
particularly mothers of preschool-age children, are
working, the majority of them full time? What does
it imply about the care children receive at home?
And what does it mean to the variety of institutions
and organizations that care for children?

The care and supervision of children for whom no

adult family member is at home during the day falls into two categories: full day care for children below school age and supplemental care for children who are in school, but for only part of their parents' working hours. Most existing studies focus on the former type of care; consequently, most of this discussion deals with day care, although we return later to the issue of care for school-age children.

Day care has diverse historical and philosophical roots. It has served as a form of care for deprived children or children of parents regarded as inadequate, designed to substitute for parental care or to offer corrective, protective, or therapeutic experiences. This rationale has become less and less appropriate as the number and kinds of children receiving daytime care have changed from a small group with special needs to a very large group of normal, healthy children. As more and more women with young children enter the labor force, it is overwhelmingly the "average" child who is participating in these programs. Although many of these children are from low-income families, increased maternal employment in two-parent families means that many children enrolled in these programs are from middle-income and upper-middle-income families as well. Hence, most day care now responds not to special problems, but to normal needs. From the parents' point of view, these services fulfill caretaking, socializing, and educational functions, regardless of their auspices.

The other historical and philosophical origins of day care are much more closely linked to its current social functions. Day care has long been regarded as an institutional arrangement designed to free mothers to work outside the home; for example, the Lanham Act passed during World War II provided federal funds on a relatively large scale to provide child care for women working in war-related industries. In the more recent past, the concept of early childhood education, especially for children from low-income families, has become legitimized through the establishment and growth of Head Start and many precursory programs. Day care centers have increasingly committed themselves to providing educational services and are frequently viewed as sources for providing developmental benefits to children.

Over time the distinction between care provided under social welfare auspices and other types of care, particularly that offered under educational auspices, has become blurred. The central aim of all types of care is to provide "good" experience, at reasonable cost, in a convenient location, that will offer a supplemental and enriching experience for children. Day care is not a substitution for parental care, because the children who are served clearly do have parents--for the most part concerned and caring parents.

Existing day care research largely falls into two categories: academic research in developmental psychology and applied or policy-related research, much of it oriented toward the agency service system and the children in it. This discussion is concerned primarily with the latter body of research. It is important to recognize how little articulation there is between the two types of research and how incomplete a picture they paint of the settings in which children receive care and of the effects of different environments on their well-being and development.

Policy-related research focuses on publicly subsidized care and examines its costs and benefits in light of the goals of particular social service systems or social policies. For example, policy analysts such as Steiner (1971) and Rivlin (1972) have examined the costs and benefits of providing child care for families receiving public assistance (AFDC) in order to allow them to work (Steiner 1971). Similarly, policy researchers such as Ditmore and Prosser (1973) have examined the effects of day care on labor force participation among low-income mothers, indicating how day care might facilitate or impede programs such as the work incentive (WIN) program. Some research that combines the policy and development traditions asks whether the day care experience reduces the developmental gap between children in poverty and other children in society (e.g., Golden et al. 1978). To date, such research has barely begun to address broader questions about the full range of day care options available to parents and children.

The National Day Care Study, carried out in 1977, illustrates some of the strengths and limitations of this research tradition. The objective of the study, funded by the Administration for Children, Youth, and Families, was to examine the impact of regulatable characteristics on the quality and cost of center care, primarily for preschool children ages 3-5. The study focused on staff/child ratios, group size, and the qualifications of service providers. Centers and sites were carefully chosen so that low-income and middle-income groups, as well as black children and white children, were adequately represented. In addition to collecting detailed cost information, the study produced an extensive body of information on the effects on children, their family backgrounds, and the expectations of their parents in choosing particular care arrangements (Ruopp et al. 1979). Results of the study have influenced the recently proposed revisions of federal day care standards for the purchase of services, thereby indicating the value of research on categorical programs. However, because the study was tailored to meet specific agency needs, it did not address several issues critical to planning future government support for day care.

First, the study did not address the relative cost and quality of family care and care in a child's own home by relatives or paid caregivers. Nor has this crucial issue received the attention it deserves in other studies. One relatively large-scale study (Golden et al. 1978) conducted in New York has addressed these questions. A few smaller studies have been published or are currently in progress (e.g., Prescott 1973, Cochran 1977, Doyle and Somers 1975), as is a large-scale descriptive study of family day care being conducted for the Administration for Children, Youth, and Families. However, a great deal of comparative work remains to be done.

Second, the National Day Care Study, like other policy studies, provides almost no information on the interaction of day care with the home environment in shaping the life of the child. Current research fails to address such questions as: to what extent does a supportive home environment reinforce the positive effects of day care or overcome a negative experience? While some research and commentary exist on parent participation and parent-caregiver relationships (Sjlund 1973; Robinson et al. 1973; Fein 1976; Powell 1977a, 1977b, 1978a, 1978b, 1979; Kamerman 1980), there are few direct investigations of the effects on children.

Third, the National Day Care Study, and policy

studies in general, have not measured the effects of multiple care arrangements on children. Many youngsters attend kindergarten or preschool for part of the day, receive group day care for other parts of the day or on alternative days, and are cared for by a baby-sitter or relative at other times. Research has provided little insight concerning the consequences of these arrangements for children, their parents, and the variety of institutions that provide substitute care.

Finally, one of the most striking limitations of policy studies and academic studies alike is their failure to consider critical age distinctions in relation to types of care. Policy studies, such as the National Day Care Study, have largely focused on children in the 3-5 age group, who often receive some form of group experience through prekindergarten or nursery schools, whether they are in day care or not. In contrast, many studies in developmental psychology have examined the effects of group or center care on much younger children because of the presumed importance of very early experience, particularly mother-child attachment, on the child's social and intellectual development (Belsky and Steinberg 1978, Etaugh 1980, Kagan 1976, Riccinti 1976). Both bodies of research have largely neglected the large group of children under 3, who receive care from family day care mothers (women who care for other children as well as their own) or from paid or unpaid substitute caregivers in their own homes as well as those of school age, who may receive care before and after school hours and during vacations in a variety of makeshift arrangements.

Other policy studies have similarly been limited in focus and have therefore been less influential than they might have been in informing policy. For example, the National Child Care Consumer Study attempted a comprehensive mapping of the demand for different types of care (UNCO 1975). However, the study followed the research tradition in this area in not tabulating kindergarten and school attendance of children ages 3-5 as child care, thus limiting substantially the worth of its report for planning purposes. It also did not make obvious distinctions in length of care, lumping casual baby-sitting with formal arrangements and creating a category of care of 10-29 hours per week, thus obscuring significant distinctions within that range.

We believe that research should proceed from a broad definition of child care, one that includes out-of-home care under many auspices and even some forms of in-home care. Future research on child care should place it in the larger contexts of the daily life of the child and family and of current social trends and governmental responses to those trends. This widening of the traditional definition will draw attention to critical issues that are not currently being addressed or that are being addressed inadequately. Examples of areas of potential policy-relevant inquiry based on this broader definition include:

* More comprehensive and accurate studies designed to specify the demand and supply of child care, taking account of the full range of care arrangements available and parental preferences for different types of care for children of different ages.

* Studies of the comparative effects on development of different care environments, taking account of the actual distribution of children across types of care by age. Such studies would include studies of the consequences of formal and informal care arrangements for children of school age and below, the consequences for the shrinking group of children ages 3-5 who do not receive some form of group experience, and the consequences of age-segregated versus age-integrated care.

* Studies of the effects of multiple forms of full-day and part-day care, including nursery school, Head Start, kindergarten, playschools, and other preschool programs as well as center care and family day care. Such studies would investigate the convenience of different mixes of care for parents, the ways in which parents resolve conflicts between

child care and work schedules, the effects of multiple forms of care on children, and redundancies or gaps in the total public and private child care service system.

• Research on the effects of day care on the well-being and functioning of parents and of the family as a unit. Existing research on the effects of day care focuses almost exclusively on direct outcomes for the child. Almost no attention has been paid to the significance of day care to parents and thereby (indirectly) to the child. Both on theoretical and experimental grounds, there are reasons for believing that such indirect influences may be of major importance and therefore should constitute a major focus of future research efforts.

• Investigation of the extent and type of public subsidy (and the level of government providing subsidy) needed to provide access to child care for families currently unable to afford it. Such studies would focus in detail on the effects of different mechanisms (e.g., direct fees for services versus vouchers) on different segments of the child care market. Studies would also investigate the interaction of state and local regulatory policies with subsidy mechanisms in determining the market response to public funding.

• Studies investigating the costs of care that distinguish between costs attributable to the core care program and those attributable to ancillary services (e.g., nutrition, counseling, or health care). The National Day Care Study found that costs of mandated ancillary services account for a large fraction of the difference in total cost between federally subsidized care and less costly parent-fee care, although the study was unable to attribute specific costs to specific supplemental services. The need for such services--hence the cost of care--varies markedly with the type of population served (poor versus middle-class groups). Moreover, ancillary services are much more widely available in center care than in other care arrangements. A full understanding of the costs of different forms of care in relation to their benefits for different populations must take account of this critical element.

• Research on the costs and benefits of not providing care: the cost to a child who may not have what is becoming the normative experience for most children; the cost to parents of trying to manage a complicated amalgam of care arrangements while coping with work and home responsibilities; the cost to women and to society of having to withdraw from the labor force for at least some portion of their lives;

and the benefits of a parent's staying at home to
care for children.

• Research on the costs and benefits to
parents, children, and society of alternative forms
of social insurance provided to families with young
children--e.g., cash subsidies to all mothers versus
subsidized child care--and on ways in which society
can support working parents without creating
disincentives for two-parent families who would
prefer to get by on a single income.

• Studies of the changing relationship between
work and family life as women enter the labor force
and of ways in which the apparent intransigence of
the workplace can be modified to enable adults to be
more productive in both domains.

Adolescence:
Services for
Youth Development

Adolescence, as a socially defined period of life,
seems to be lasting longer for many young people.
Teenagers are experiencing greater social
independence from their parents as patterns of family
care change. The increasingly earlier onset of
physical maturity, the accelerating entry of mothers

into the work force, the increasing numbers of single-parent families, the access of young teenagers to automobiles, and patterns of peer interaction that take teenagers out of the home for extended periods seem to have resulted in a reduction in close parental supervision of adolescents. At the same time, the expansion of higher education and the rise in unemployment of young people have held back their entry into the competitive labor market and thus held them in an independent adult status. For certain groups of adolescents, particularly black and Hispanic males, difficulty in getting jobs has become a prominent national issue. The broader underlying issue is the extended dependency of adolescents generally, which leaves them in a kind of limbo with no tasks to perform and few options for using their time.

As the Panel on Youth of the President's Science Advisory Committee noted, when America was still primarily an agrarian society, the needs of youth were "necessarily subordinate to the economic struggle, and the occupational requisites permitted them to be brought quickly into adult productivity." The dominant institutional settings in which young people grew up were the home and workplace, and parents generally exemplified the future roles of their children. In short, socialization was accomplished through continual interaction with parents and nearby adults. But as society evolved through the 20th century, a long period of formal training with specialized instruction was initiated. As a consequence, the world of the maturing child, formerly dominated by the home, became dominated by the school at the formal level and by the peer group at the informal level (Panel on Youth of the President's Science Advisory Committee 1974).

Reduced supervision by the family and a reduced impact of the world of work on older adolescents has changed the experience of adolescence. Peers, social institutions, and the broader community have become more influential. Advertising has fostered and sustained the notion of a separate teenage culture, with distinct patterns of consumption, recreation, and peer associations. Research on the effect of these larger forces on youth is unequivocal in affirming their importance, but knowledge about how youth interact with the institutions and communities surrounding them is sparse (Hill 1973).

We do not know enough about what contemporary adolescent lives are like. We can sense what may be missing from the lives of many young people--e.g., close family supports, clear paths to the adult world--but our knowledge of the forces that have replaced them in importance is inadequate, as is our knowledge of the way adolescents interact with the numerous programs available to them. This lack of knowledge hinders the design of programs that hold some promise of benefiting youth. It also gives rise to the perception, frequently encountered in schools and juvenile courts, that the youth being served are alienated from many community norms and relationships.

All levels of government are being pressed to assume greater responsibility for services to adolescents who are termed "high-risk" youth or "youth with special needs" for whom traditional services have apparently not worked. The Juvenile Justice and Delinquency Prevention Act of 1974 emphasized a movement away from the provisions of children's services in residential institutions toward supervision at home or in residential community environments such as halfway houses and outreach centers. As a stipulation for states to receive federal funds (specifically from the Office of Juvenile Justice and Delinquency Prevention), the act mandates deinstitutionalization of status offenders and of dependent and neglected children through reductions in the rates at which these populations are institutionalized. It prohibits the incarceration or detention of juvenile offenders in adult correctional facilities, the commingling of delinquents and status offenders, and the institutionalization and commingling of dependent and neglected children. Though no federal laws have been enacted to mandate the deinstitutionalization of mentally impaired children, several lower court rulings have upheld the principle of maintaining these children in "least restrictive" environments

(Wyatt v. Stickney 1971, New York State Association for Retarded Children v. Carey 1975).

The emphasis on deinstitutionalization has brought many children who were not ordinarily part of the service system or who were cared for previously in isolated residential facilities into supervisory settings closer to the mainstream of community life. In so doing, it has stimulated expansion of publicly financed home and community-based services to meet the special needs of these children and their families.

The full effects of this change in the pattern of services to youth are not yet understood, but several trends are emerging. First, the effort to avoid institutional care of youth may have resulted in more of them coming under public jurisdiction. At least in some states, the growth of programs to divert youth from the penalties of the juvenile justice system has increased the overall number of youth in the public purview; for example, those who once were sent home by police are now referred to a "diversion" program. Second, many observers believe that the movement away from residential care has brought many adolescents and pre-adolescents with severe behavioral disturbances into the child welfare system, thereby placing special demands on child welfare and educational institutions. There has been an increase in the number and rate of placements of children in various forms of foster care. According to a recent national survey of children's services, a significant proportion of children referred for foster care or other traditional child welfare services were identified as status offenders and juvenile delinquents by the court, the probation officer, or the police (Shyne and Schroeder 1978). Between 1960 and 1974 the rate of placement of children in foster care increased from 3.7 to 4.7 per 1,000 of the population. There has also been an expansion of care in group homes, from a 1970 capacity of 4,800 children nationally to a capacity of 6,000 in 30 states (excluding New York and California) in 1974 (Wiltse 1978). In addition, there has been a proliferation of special community-based social and educational programs for the mentally retarded, the mentally impaired, and for the vaguely defined category, "youth with special needs." The nature, extent, and value of these new service programs are little understood.

Programs associated with the trend toward deinstitutionalization are not the only evidence of growing government involvement in services to adolescents. A variety of programs provides vocational and employment training and job opportunities to unemployed youth, treatment and education to young drug and alcohol abusers, and treatment and counseling to pregnant teenagers. However, these programs are focused on specific target groups labeled by reference to their most highly visible problem: delinquents, status offenders, foster children, unemployed youth, substance abusers, teenage parents, etc. Most programs reach only a fraction of those who could benefit from them, and the vast majority of existing services do not take a developmental approach. They do not encourage continuity from childhood to adulthood and do not promote the notion of healthy development based on recognition of social, cultural, intellectual, and emotional differences among adolescents in different social and economic circumstances.

The prevailing view of an appropriate strategy for youth services has not always been so narrow as it is now. Broader lines of thought on youth services can actually be identified in the early work of Shaw and his colleagues (1929) on the influence of delinquent subcultures and the relationship of these subcultures to the broader community. Similarly, in the late 1950s and early 1960s, the work of Cloward and Ohlin (1964), Spergel (1964), and other researchers investigating patterns of delinquent youth behavior stressed the close and subtle ties of youth to the institutions and social agencies that surrounded them as well as to the social norms of these surroundings. Their problems were then perceived as reflections of social problems defined in the broadest sense; the way to change youth behavior was to change society. Attempts were made to translate this thinking into

operational strategies, first in local demonstration
projects and then in national policy. (The Youth
Development and Delinquency Prevention Act of 1961
grew, to some extent, from this line of thought.)

Yet this broad view of youth and their problems
proved difficult to sustain in policy and program
terms, because it dealt with youth services primarily
in terms of large-scale social change. The
difficulties in accomplishing such change have proved
immense, and the public commitment to such change has
been variable.

Research has not pictured adolescence as one phase
in a continuing developmental process. Researchers
have tended to focus on the typical psychological and
maturational changes of this stage of life. Funding
and programming for both research and services have
concentrated on the adolescent problems that have
dominated public and voluntary activities with
adolescents. There is a large research emphasis on
delinquency and crime, pregnancy, drug use, alcohol-
ism, and employment. There has been insufficient
research oriented at the larger, more basic question
of the role of adolescence in American society.

To obtain knowledge that can help define the
appropriate level and form of public responsibilities
for youth, investigations of the social nature of
adolescence must supplement individual-oriented
findings. A research agenda in this area should
maintain an intermediate course between a broad

approach focused solely on institutional and social changes--over which public policy has little influence--and a narrow approach focused on the individual--which may be ineffective. The research agenda we outline below makes four main suggestions for research: research on the social context and incidence of specific behaviors among adolescents; research on patterns of family care for adolescents and the impact of public intervention on the family; research on the effectiveness of new community-based service delivery systems; and research on the issue of adolescent emancipation.

Research on the Social Context and Incidence of Specific Behaviors Among Adolescents

If we are correct in assuming basic changes in the nature of adolescence, an initial step for research is to build a greater understanding of the impact of these changes on the lives of young people. The research we suggest focuses on learning more about the day-to-day experiences and perceptions of adolescents. Not only do we need to know more about the interactions of adolescents with their families and peers and in schools, but we also should study their interactions with public and private agencies, with informal networks of community support, and with disruptive community conditions. More investigation of the changing economic role played by adolescents within their families would also be valuable. To what extent do youths in different social groups work at part-time jobs, and how do they spend the money earned? If both parents or the single parent is working, to what degree are family needs (e.g., child-care and household needs) fulfilled by the children and adolescents? To what extent do children of different ages still contribute to family businesses and farms through their labor? What is the impact of such work on the adjustment of families and children and on their use of and need for agency services? How do these economic activities affect the lives of children and relate to changing definitions of adolescence?

Examination of specific types of behavior and experiences among adolescents would also have great utility in planning youth services. What is now interpreted as problem behavior among some adolescents who come to the attention of public authorities may be typical behavior, characteristic of adolescents of all social and economic back-grounds. Self-reported data by adolescents tend to support this view, indicating that minor misbehaviors and mild delinquent behavior are widespread among youth. Research on the nature and prevalence of misbehavior in school, running away, minor crimes against property, and so forth could provide a basis for identifying behaviors that raise public concern and require intervention whether they are typical or not.

Much of what now seems to be an increase in minor juvenile misbehaviors may in fact be harmless, quite common behavior when examined within a broader understanding of adolescence. On the other hand, serious, violent criminal activity among youth appears to be growing (Strasberg 1978), and public agencies in most states report an increase in the number of adolescents who exhibit destructive behavior and extreme conflicts with family, schools, and courts. It can be argued that for these youth, the period of adolescence establishes the range of adult vocational options and determines subsequent antisocial patterns.

Research related to these adolescents has two aims: the identification of demographic and behavioral characteristics of youth who cause severe damage to themselves and others and analysis of the effects of conditions experienced in adolescence over time. The behavior of many young people is disruptive to the community as well as to their own social and intellectual development. There are now few empirical data on the characteristics of "high risk" youth who exhibit violent, destructive, and antisocial behaviors. A suggested first step for descriptive research is to define this group and identify the characteristics of youth who are perceived as placing new burdens on public services.

To identify forms of intervention in adolescence that can make a difference in adult life, longitudinal studies are suggested to track the effect of major life experiences and of various interventions on subsequent adult patterns. Research over time on target groups such as foster children, youth who act out in schools, and youth who commit violent crimes could begin to identify those characteristics that should receive program response.

Research on Patterns of Family Care for Adolescents and the Impact of Public Intervention on the Family

As public responsibility for supervision, support, and assistance to youth continues to increase, there is growing concern about the effect of this expansion on family care of adolescents. Ultimately this question must be examined at two levels: How does an expansion of public support for certain categories of youth (for example, handicapped youth or mentally impaired youth) alter the general pattern of family care? And how do service interventions on behalf of an adolescent affect his or her family support? To some extent, recommending research in this area is anticipatory. The usual pattern would be to expand public responsibility for a target population and then, retrospectively, examine its effect on family patterns and on behavior. We suggest instead that demonstrations and experimental research intended to measure the effects of promising interventions be initiated to guide the likely expansion of public services for youth.

Key issues involve the activities and especially

the responsibilities that are expected of adolescents in different segments of American society. A widely held view is that participation in responsible activities serves to counteract problem behavior, but the phenomenon has not been sufficiently researched. Investigations along this line are of high priority.

A related topic requiring systematic study is the availability of adults in the lives of adolescents. Adult participation, which is seen as a constructive force in the development of teenagers, is being reduced as a function of decreasing adult volunteerism. As more parents, both mothers and fathers, work outside the home, they are not available to participate in the activities of adolescents. Such roles as scout leader, which have traditionally been filled by parents or other adults on a volunteer basis, are either remaining unfilled or are being filled by paid service providers. Both the extent and the role of adult participation in the lives of adolescents should be subjects of further research.

Research on the Effectiveness of New Community-Based Service Delivery Systems

The pressure to produce community-based services has resulted in many new programs and agencies for youth. These agencies claim an increasing proportion of public and private service dollar, but almost no sound evaluative research is available on their performance. To a great extent, the responsibility to produce this research should rest with the public sector, yet the strength of the existing public policy commitment to these new, community-based programs suggests that the private sector should support research in this area as well, since its efforts are unbiased by prior policy decisions.

Research on the Issue of Adolescent Emancipation

Many of the current issues relating to parental consent for medical service, independent living, receipt of transfer payments, and labor-market policy are premised on views of the age of emancipation--the age at which youth are able and are allowed to make their own decisions about their actions and well-being--or differential emancipation by issue or domain. Research is needed to provide an empirical base for consideration of such questions in a policy context.

Our suggestions include both basic research and evaluation. Little knowledge currently exists concerning adolescent decision making. In designing interventions it would be useful to know much more than we do about the nature and quality of the decisions adolescents make when they are "emancipated"--who influences them, what weight is given to the future consequences of their choices, etc. as well as how these factors vary among adolescents at different ages. Such research could

include the evaluation of youth service bureaus,
youth advocacy agencies, nontraditional networks for
youth that have emerged in urban areas, and
coalitions of informal service providers that have
developed as the result of recent public and private
financing.

Financing Children's Services:
Tracing Costs and Benefits

As noted above, in 1935 child welfare services
provided under the Social Security Act were supported
by approximately $1.5 million in federal funds
through grants-in-aid to the states; in 1977, more
than $1 billion in federal funds was allocated to
these services under Title IV and Title XX alone
(U.S. Office of Management and Budget 1977).
Although data concerning the proportion of federal,
state, local, and private funds expended for
children's services in each of the states are
unavailable, studies done in Ohio, Illinois, and
Massachusetts indicate that a combination of federal
grants and state and local tax revenues comprise the
dominant source of supply (Case Western Reserve
University 1977, Sheehan 1977).

With this increase in public funding, private (or
voluntary) child welfare agencies have become more
dependent on government support for two reasons.

First, private agencies have found it increasingly
difficult to finance their programs from voluntary
funds alone and have relied on public funds to meet
their rising costs. Second, since the late 1960s, as
federal categorical programs specifying types of
service and delivery have become more prominent,
states have tended to rely on the purchase of
services from private agencies. When state
administrative structures prevent public agencies
from delivering services or when specialized
services, such as abortion counseling, are required
by specific client groups, state officials have found
greater flexibility in subsidizing the private sector
than in delivering services directly through their
own agencies. This is also true when voluntary
interest groups are strong in certain areas of
service delivery, as, for example, are the United Way
and the Child Welfare League of America; they
advocate public subsidies and the purchase of
services (Haring 1976). Significantly, however, the
current strategy of using general tax revenues to
support children's services, particularly child
welfare services, has made it difficult to trace
expenditures and to know exactly what public
resources are buying.

Complete data concerning public support of
services delivered by private child welfare agencies
in each state are unavailable. However, 90 voluntary
agencies for which comparable data are available for

1960 and 1975 showed an average increase from 28 percent to 57 percent in the proportion of their income derived from government sources (Haring 1976). In Illinois, for example, private voluntary agencies serving children derive between one-third and one-half of their funding from government sources. In New York City, 85-95 percent of the operating budgets of the nearly 90 agencies serving children are supported by public funds. Moreover, voluntary child welfare agencies were deriving 90 percent of their budgets from public sources in 1978, while voluntary family service centers were deriving 22 percent of their budgets from public sources.

In a very real sense, the method of financing services for children drives the system. Budgeting allocations determine who gets services; the long-established pattern of grants and contracts often determines which agencies deliver services; the priorities associated with financing create incentives that influence the type of services provided; and the amount of financing influences the level and quality of the services. In this regard, several pioneering studies have attempted to describe patterns of expenditures at the federal and state levels. For example, as a part of a larger study of federal programs and policies related to children, Ruth Rose of Harvard University presented a scheme for categorizing expenditures according to whether programs were intended to benefit only children or to benefit children as a part of a larger population (e.g., families, the mentally ill). Programs were also categorized according to whether they were intended to benefit children directly by providing cash and social services or whether they benefit children indirectly by providing technical assistance, training, and research support (Rose 1976).

"Children's budgets," which attempt to trace the flow of funds from the federal government through the states to the point of service delivery, have been developed for Ohio, North Carolina, and Illinois, and one is now being developed for New York City by researchers at Columbia University.[7] The National Institute of Education has recently supported a more ambitious effort to develop a national youth budget.[8] The purposes of the research are: (1) to examine the changing scale and nature of federal expenditures for youth by conducting a longitudinal analysis; (2) to examine equity in the distribution of federal expenditures for youth by comparing the geographic

[7]Charles Brecher and Raymond Horton, senior research associates at the Center of Conservation of Human Resources, Columbia University, are developing a children's budget for New York City with support from the Ford Foundation.

[8]Brecher and Horton (see note 6) are carrying out the Youth Budget Project, supported by the National Institute of Education.

distribution of resources with the distribution of children; (3) to examine the nature and scale of total public expenditures for youth; and (4) to measure efficiency in the delivery of services to youth by analyzing the cost structure of these services.

These studies have found it a major effort merely to identify the patterns of fund disbursement from federal to state to local levels of government and to identify which services are financed with what funds. The lack of data partially explains the lack of research attention to financing issues. In addition, service financing is usually considered a narrow economic issue. For example, much of the available research on the financing of children's services consists of cost-benefit studies that evaluate alternative program strategies for foster care, day care, and institutional care, etc., in comparison to community-based services. The costs considered in these analyses have been the direct dollar expenditures by the state or local government or by the private sector.

Examination of service financing in this way can be useful, particularly if the goal is to clarify a practical range of program choices. However, choices framed in these terms--that is, within the framework of an existing service system--do not promote an examination of the benefits of one service sector in comparison to another. Nor can such analyses provide information on how decisions about resource allocation are made. As long as financing is thought of only as a technical aspect of the existing system of services, there is little possibility for a comprehensive review of how public responsibility for children is financed and discharged.

Financing should be viewed not only as a disbursement of funds but as the embodiment of decisions on how to carry out society's responsibility for children. This perspective suggests a number of research issues.

Basic to any analysis of the efficacy of children's services is a comparison of the stated intentions of service programs with the services actually financed under these programs. This type of analysis has been undertaken within specific programs, but rarely at levels that enable the actual uses of service resources to be evaluated against the broad public goals that these resources are expected to accomplish.

Financing children's services involves a complex process of choice influenced by program guidelines, the pattern of intergovernmental relationships, and political realities as well as professional decisions on effective service interventions. There is surprisingly little research that documents how service financing and budgeting are accomplished or why certain decisions are made rather than others.

A first step in building a greater understanding

of these decision-making processes could include studies of the budgeting processes of state governments, particularly the processes by which financing for children's service is negotiated in relation to financing for other target groups; the process by which public finances are allocated to private agencies rather than to direct delivery by public agencies; and the degree to which executive and legislative decision makers are aware of the results inherent in their decision making.

One of the most rapid changes in children's service financing has been the shift from private to predominantly public financing. The long-standing control of children's services by private agencies is changing, largely because the bulk of financing for these agencies now comes from public funds. Although this change is acknowledged as a key factor in the nature of service delivery and has been documented by the Child Welfare League of America and others, its implications are little understood. Two types of research seem useful here. Policy researchers could examine such issues as: the incentives created by public financing and how private delivery systems respond to these incentives as well as the nature of the authority exercised by a private agency when it is supported by public funds but governed by a private board. Empirical research and data gathering are needed on such issues as the extent to which residual private financing for children's services shapes service delivery; the extent to which the influx of public money has driven out private financing; and the effect of public financing, both direct expenditures and tax expenditures, on informal service networks and supports for children and on services provided in the marketplace. The current patterns of children's service financing have been so well established that little research attention has been given to alternative methods of financing. Alternative financing mechanisms have been suggested for public education, e.g., a voucher system that would provide parents cash or coupons redeemable at several different schools for educational services, thus allowing parents to select the learning environment for their children. One alternative for children's services does, in fact, exist, in the form of the income tax credit for the purchase of child care services. It is possible that other alternative financing methods could be effective in other areas as well. Both the voucher mechanism and a refundable tax credit could be worth testing for child welfare services as well as for youth services. Providing more direct control to families over the service they receive may promote a different level of participation.

Current measures of the effectiveness of public program expenditures have focused on the direct costs and benefits of service provision. Cost-benefit analyses, however, have generally ignored the costs

to families and society of not providing services--
for example, the opportunity costs to a parent who
refuses employment outside the home because adequate
child care is unavailable or the costs to society of
providing long-term care to a mentally retarded
individual who was not provided the necessary basic
training to improve his or her self-sufficiency.
Similarly, analyses have often focused only on the
direct benefits of interventions, thereby missing
important outcomes, such as the strengthening of
informal helping networks as a result of early
education programs that require parental
participation. In addition, not only have such
analyses frequently focused on the short-term costs
of providing services or of providing services versus
cash benefits, but also they have not given adequate
attention to the long-term costs of alternative
interventions. Future analyses of public service
financing should include measures of the costs to
parents, communities, and society of providing or not
providing particular services. They should take into
account both direct benefits to children and indirect
benefits to their families and other institutions
participating in their care.

AN AGENDA
FOR RESEARCH

Children are dependent on a wide variety of people, institutions, and circumstances in their daily lives. Publicly financed services are only a part--usually only a small part--of the child's environment. To study children's problems and needs only in narrow, program-specific contexts is to miss a vital point: the effectiveness of these services depends on how they relate to the overall environment in which children live.

In our discussions of child care, youth services, and public financing of children's services, we have tried to show that focusing on children rather than on agencies and programs leads to more fundamental questions concerning children's needs and the ways in which statutory and publicly financed services can meet those needs. Child care may better be approached as a broad range of formal and informal activities contributing to the care and development of children, rather than as the daytime maintenance of youngsters in the child welfare system. Adolescent services, now established as categorical programs to curb juvenile delinquency, teenage drug abuse, youth unemployment, and the like, may better be conceived as activities organized to support a healthy transition from childhood to adulthood. The financing of children's services may more appropriately be recognized as the product of a complex process of choice involving the allocation of time, money, and human resources among a wide variety of public and private, formal and informal activities.

These examples indicate that future research and analysis concerning policy on children's services requires the development of a strong base of empirical knowledge concerning children's lives. We need to learn much more than we now know about the actual experiences of children and their families in different segments of society. For example, where are they living? What are the conditions of their homes, neighborhoods, and communities, including their schools, churches, parks, playgrounds, and the other important places where they go? How do children spend their time out of school and in what environments? Who are the important people in their lives, including parents, siblings, extended family friends, and caretakers outside the family? What do these people do for children, when, and where?

Future studies should be more informative as to how children's needs vary with differences in environment or context. For example, what are the differences in children's needs between low-income and middle-income households, between single-parent and two-parent households, between one-earner families and two-earner families, between families under stress (e.g., from serious illness, separation, or unemployment) and those not under stress, and between rural, urban, and suburban settings? How does a child's age affect these subcultural differences? All children require food, shelter, clothing, and health care. They also are presumed to benefit from the continuous involvement of one or more loving and concerned adults. Yet certain environments are more supportive of a child's healthy development than others. How do social conditions affect the ability of a child's family to meet these needs or the ability of others outside the family to provide for his or her care? Which needs are not being met? How do children whose needs are not met within the family or by social programs cope? What alternative mechanisms are available to them? To what extent and under what circumstances do they benefit or are they adversely affected?

New information is needed on services, highlighting how services in different systems complement or conflict with one another. Because families generally rely on a variety of supports, it is important to understand how these supports vary among different sectors of society and among different societies and how they improve the contexts in which children live. New information can be gained from research on children, families, and services in other countries. Although we have not attempted a systematic review of the status of research on services for children outside the United States, an agenda for strengthened research on children's services would certainly include topics that would benefit from cross-national transfer of data and findings.[9]

A range of questions awaits further research efforts: to what extent are children from different social and economic circumstances dependent on the state to meet their needs? How does that dependency affect their capacity to become self-sufficient adults? How does the availability and/or imposition of government aid and support affect the availability of services provided in other systems, such as kin

---

[9]Some studies that we are aware of include an examination by Kahn and Kamerman of income packages potentially available to 15 family types in 8 countries; a study supported by the Foundation for Child Development in which children and parents in France and Japan are being interviewed about critical aspects of their experiences; and a cross-national longitudinal study by Bronfenbrenner of formal and informal community support systems and service networks.

and community networks? And how do entrenched organizational patterns and professional practices, such as those characteristic of schools, social work agencies, and health care agencies, constrain opportunities for redirecting or reorganizing service delivery?

Suggested
Topics for
Research

Child care, youth services, and public financing are by no means the only important issues for future research. Indeed, for the existing system of public services to be redirected in ways that increase its capacity to enhance children's normal and healthy development, future research should address a number of major themes and topics, of which the following list is suggestive but by no means exhaustive.

The Role of the Schools in the Provision of Children's Services

Schools have traditionally defined their role as the provision of academic education--the development of cognitive skills such as reading, writing, and mathematical reasoning. Yet as we understand the circumstances that mitigate the ability of teachers to teach and students to learn, issues are raised concerning the provision of services in schools other than basic instruction. Research has shown that services such as nutrition, medical care, recreation, and psychological counseling may significantly affect a child's ability to perform well in the classroom. Similarly, the Education for all Handicapped Children Act has highlighted the importance of a variety of other ancillary services, such as transportation and the provision of special facilities and instruction to all children with handicaps or other special needs. As more and more mothers of school-age and preschool-age children enter the labor force, it seems likely that schools will more frequently be called on to provide child care and after-school programs, although the extent of such demand is not known. Moreover, as the problems of adolescents are better understood, many parents and experts look to the schools to provide numerous noncognitive activities deemed valuable to youth development, such as extracurricular programs, vocational and work-related programs, and community projects. How effective schools are in providing these more diverse services is influenced by the training and preparation that school personnel receive.

Future research should explore the potential role of the schools in providing services other than academic instruction, examining the variety of demands on schools for services, the extent to which these services are currently being provided under other auspices, and the kinds of problems that would arise in relocating these services in schools. One of the issues involved is the extent to which teachers and other school personnel are adequately trained to provide services beyond academic instruction. Future studies should measure the relative costs and benefits of expanding the role of the schools in service provision. They should explore the costs of providing these services in the schools versus other social service settings and the costs of not providing them at all. Moreover, research should explore the effects of diverting schools from their traditional functions. To the extent that children's and their parents' perceptions of the role of the schools is altered, is the effectiveness of these institutions and their traditional service providers in teaching cognitive skills adversely affected?

Public Supports for Parenthood

As we have emphasized throughout this report, publicly financed children's services mandated by statute are predominantly addressed to children's isolated problems and needs--for example, retardation, abuse, sickness, educational deprivation, and delinquency. Yet children's problems may, in fact, be a direct reflection of their parents' inability to perform their child-rearing functions. To the extent that parents are in need of assistance, children frequently are, too. Some public programs are aimed at helping families.

Aid to Families with Dependent Children (AFDC) provides cash to eligible families. The Work Incentive Program (WIN) provides jobs, job training, and some related day care services for parents who are poor, unskilled, and unemployed. Medicaid provides health services to poor families. Social Security provides social insurance in cases of death or disability and survivor benefits to young people up to the age of 23 who are in school. Yet each of these programs is aimed at a particular problem or problems, and rather than complement one another they frequently conflict in important respects. To the extent that one program eases the burden of poverty, it may cause a parent or family to become ineligible for benefits provided by another program or for other public services directed to children. In many cases these programs and services inhibit the ability of parents to obtain aid and support through other systems--for example kin and community networks--by the way they define eligibility.

Future research should explore the needs of families in a variety of circumstances as well as the extent to which public programs directly aid or do not aid parents. They should also examine the extent to which public programs and other interventions support or do not support the effective functioning of informal service systems. For example, how do

factors such as television influence parents'
perceptions of their roles as parents and facilitate
or impede their functioning? A major question
concerning public supports for parenthood is what
constitutes a good or helpful intervention. If
helpful programs can be envisioned, how do we measure
their costs and benefits?

The Appropriate Role of the State in Protecting the Best Interests of the Child

In recent decades the relationship between the
state, the parent, and the child has shifted. As a
result of both legislative enactments and court
decisions, the state has assumed greater responsibility and jurisdiction over minor children.
Available data indicate that the states are
increasingly intervening in families in which
parents' ability to care for their children is
unclear; two examples are cases of child abuse and
status offenders. In many situations parents no
longer have autonomy to decide what is in the best
interest of their children--for example, to refuse
medical treatment of a child who is ill, to
discipline children as they see fit, to refuse
services and counseling provided as a package of
benefits, or to maintain jurisdiction over a child
declared in need of special supervision.

The recent trend toward ever broader
interpretations of children's rights has had a

similar effect. It can be argued that most recent government decisions, such as those concerning a minor's right to obtain an abortion without parental permission, are in fact further expansions of the state's rights at the expense of parents' rights rather than expansions of children's rights. In the end, for example, it is the courts and social service agencies--not a young girl or her parents--that have authority to decide whether she can obtain an abortion if she is unable to pay for it herself.

Future studies should explore the implications of this changing relationship between the state, the parent, and the child. To what extent is in fact jurisdiction and responsibility for protecting the best interests of children shifting away from parents? How does this relationship vary across states and localities? Research should also examine the effect of this changing relationship on parents in their role as parents and in their relationship to their children. Do parents view themselves as more dependent on outside agencies in raising their children? Do children have altered perceptions of their dependency on their parents? Future studies should examine the extent to which this changing relationship, or the perception of it, has influenced children's needs and affected the ways in which they are served. Has it increased the demand for services outside the family? Has it also affected the quality of care and services children receive? For example,

in states in which public jurisdiction has brought
more children into the system than can be adequately
cared for, have public services harmed children more
than they have helped them? Where the courts, in
particular, have been unable to cope with the
overload, what other public agencies have become
involved and with what effects on the children being
served?

Levels of Government in the Provision of
Children's Services

Government at all levels--federal, state, and
local--is involved in the provision of chidren's
services. Neighborhoods also play a significant role
in service delivery. As more federal funds have been
provided and as more programs have been authorized by
statute, the federal role has expanded relative to
that of other levels of government. Yet primary
responsibility for the direct delivery of services to
children and their families has remained in the
states and localities. Federal funds are allocated
by a variety of mechanisms--among them block grants,
revenue sharing, and matching grants--each entailing
different degrees of federal jurisdiction over the
expenditure of funds. The states rely heavily on
federal monies to support their programs, although
the implications of this growing dependence for state
and local control over the content and management of
services are not clearly understood.

Future research on children's services should examine the distribution of responsibility for serving children among different government levels. To what extent do federal funds and the regulations governing their disbursement provide leverage to state and local governments in supporting services for children? To what extent do state and local agencies maintain jurisdiction over services despite the increasing infusion of federal funding? How do neighborhood-based services fare under overlapping jurisdictions of other levels of governance? How does the distribution of public responsibility for serving children affect the availability of services and the quality of care provided?

Alternative Services for Children

In many communities a variety of alternative services have developed to meet the special needs of children who are not always well served through regular organizational channels. Among the most visible of these are communes, runaway houses and drop-in centers, which provide shelter and counseling for non-offender youth. Alternative schools have also been developed in many communities to provide educational environments that offer greater freedom than regular schools in academic studies and the scheduling of activities. For the most part, these alternative services have experimented with antiorganizational forms that emphasize a democratic relationship between caretakers and clients, teachers and students. All members of the community participate in decision making affecting roles and routines.

The scope and potential effectiveness of various alternative services for children are not clearly understood. These programs have generally been short-lived--less than two years for most alternative schools, for example. Although it is frequently recognized that these programs perform important functions not performed by formal institutional services, they have had difficulty attracting sufficient financial support to keep them going. Because typically they do not adhere to the eligibility requirements and operational guidelines that encumber public monies, they have not received federal, state, or local funding. Moreover, although committed to the mission of their alternative programs, many service providers have proven to be unsophisticated administrators and fund raisers.

Future research on children's services should include studies of alternative services. Although it is often believed that these programs provide significant benefits to the children they serve, actual treatment effects have not been adequately measured. What can these services accomplish? In what settings do they most effectively meet children's needs? Which children are best served?

How do they complement or conflict with other publicly and privately provided services?

The Development of Standards for Children's Services

As more specialized programs have been legislated at the federal and state levels and as more public funds have been committed to providing services for children, pressure has been growing to ensure that children are well cared for and that public monies are well spent. In many cases the result has been the development of standards to regulate service delivery at the local level. Standards of practice have been established for almost all publicly supported services, including day care, foster care, education for the poor or handicapped, health care, nutrition and feeding, etc. Yet the content of standards has frequently raised numerous questions concerning their function as mechanisms to ensure quality control and accountability. Should regulations require optimal levels of care even when such standards are impractical and unenforceable? Or should they reflect practical norms that, though not optimal, are attainable and will ensure better care for children than if no standards existed? The issue is one of formulation. As in the case of the Federal Interagency Day Care requirements, child development researchers and many parents and taxpayers would argue for regulations that require the "best" care known. Service administrators and practitioners, on the other hand, would argue for regulations that require the "best" care that can reasonably be provided.

Future research should aid in the formulation of standards of service delivery. By providing knowledge of the conditions under which children live and their needs, it can also help to identify levels of care that both constitute benefits for children and are attainable. How do various standards of practice affect the adequacy and efficiency of service delivery? Are different levels of care required for children under different circumstances? How does the establishment of standards and regulations affect the availability of sevices in different systems and children's access to them?

Future Support for
Research on
Children's Services

Where should support for this kind of research come from? Who should do the research?

Empirical studies reflecting broad perspectives on children's services already represent a growing component of the research literature. In general these studies have been sponsored by private foundations and a handful of federal policy-making offices and agencies whose primary function is to support social research and development rather than to promote specific programmatic interests. This kind of work has not, as a rule, received support from mission agencies charged with administering the numerous programs directed to children and their families.

Most research on children's services is performed by university-based researchers, private for-profit and nonprofit research corporations, public interest or advocacy organizations, and in-house government research and analysis shops. Different incentives prevail in each setting, and these differences in incentives are reflected in the styles of investigation, types of research products, and perceived audiences for the researcher's work that are characteristic of each setting.

University-based researchers, for example, place a high value on methodological rigor and sophistication and on contributions to specific disciplines. They tend to avoid general exploratory studies, broad descriptions of service processes, extensive, "low-level" data collection efforts, and broad interdisciplinary studies. Moreover, because academic researchers are cautious in drawing conclusions or making recommendations on the basis of limited evidence or in the presence of major uncertainties, they are less interested in addressing the immediate questions of policy makers.

Private for-profit or nonprofit contract research

organizations, which are structured and staffed to perform both large-scale, long-term data collection and short-term policy analysis, have the capability to respond quickly to the information needs of government officials and therefore tend to structure their studies to appeal to the interests of policy makers and program managers. These performers are more involved in data collection and analysis, evaluation research, and the design of demonstrations than they are in theoretical or methodological investigations.

Studies conducted by researchers in public interest and advocacy organizations tend to be deliberately forensic in nature. Their intent is to influence decision makers at the federal and state levels to adopt their recommendations on issues regarding children's services, and they often gather information with a particular slant.

Research conducted by government agencies tends to be of several types. First, researchers in statistical agencies, such as the Bureau of the Census or the Bureau of Labor Statistics, generally perform special analyses of official data. Their reports are intended to inform decision makers, but they are also meant to be of value to the larger research community. Researchers in policy-making offices conduct studies directed at informing the short-term policy and program choices of agency decision makers. Their studies may take the form of synthetic reviews of existing research that bears on a particular policy question or analyses of data collected by others. Researchers in state and local government agencies are often engaged primarily in designing demonstrations intended to develop and promote the adoption of innovative methods of service delivery or in conducting program evaluations.

If research on children's services is to move in the new directions we are recommending, research support agencies and performers with the appropriate incentives must be recruited to the effort. Thus, achieving the new understanding we advocate presents a significant problem of organization, for there is no single research support agency and no single performer community capable of responding in the appropriate way. Several agencies and communities must recognize the unique contributions they are capable of making. To be sure, federal, state, and local mission agencies, which provide the bulk of the support for research on children's services, should broaden their perspectives on how best to fulfill their programmatic mandates and be less defensive and parochial in their research orientations. Even a small reallocation of their effort could give major impetus to the broader research we are advocating. But their missions will ultimately limit how far these agencies can go in new directions. In the same vein, performers oriented to smaller-scale disciplinary and theoretical investigations cannot be relied on for undertaking large-scale, long-term data collection, analysis, and management, nor are performers skilled in the latter types of activities likely to be independently capable of creating more powerful and fruitful theories and methodological approaches.

In contrast, foundations and those government organizations and offices whose primary activity is the support of research are not nearly so constrained, and it is to them that we must look for innovations in research on children's services. For example, federal program agencies that support research must recognize their comparative advantage in providing financial support for large-scale, longitudinal data collection. More nonprogrammatic organizations such as the National Science Foundation must recognize their unique role in stimulating creative conceptual and methodological studies that provide the basis for high-quality empirical investigations. Foundations can play a unique role in promoting high-quality, interdisciplinary research and in supporting promising research entrepreneurs and innovators.

For all society's efforts to identify and remedy children's special needs and for all of our efforts to identify available services, trace funds through the system, and evaluate treatments and programs, we--the community of policy makers and researchers concerned with children--are missing a major point.

The efficacy of everything we do on behalf of children depends in a crucial way on the environments in which children develop. Children are dependent on all the people, institutions, and circumstances that surround and influence them. Attempts to help them through provision of specific, narrowly focused services may be completely annulled by oppressive surroundings, or they may be completely misguided because of ignorance concerning the role that parents, teachers, or other people, institutions, and services play in a child's life. It would be a shame and a waste if we could not in fact help young people because we did not know enough about them and how they live to be helpful. We look at children through dozens of special lenses, yet we may never see the child. The broader vision must come from the community of researchers concerned with children's services.

REFERENCES

Belsky, J., and Steinberg, L. (1978) The effects of
    day care: a critical review. Child Development
    49:929-949.
Bradshaw, J., and Piachaud, D. (1980) Child Support
    in the European Community. London: Bedford Square
    Press.
Bronfenbrenner, U. (1979) The Ecology of Human
    Development: Experiments by Nature and Design.
    Cambridge, Mass.: Harvard University Press.
Case Western Reserve University (1977) Ohio
    Children's Budget Project. Cleveland, Ohio: Case
    Western Reserve University.
Children's Defense Fund (1977) EPSDT: Does It Spell
    Care for Poor Children. Washington, D.C.:
    Washington Research Project.
Cloward, R., and Ohlin, L. (1964) Delinquency and
    Opportunity. Glencoe, Ill.: Free Press.
Cochran, M. (1977) A comparison of group day and
    family childrearing patterns in Sweden. Child
    Development 48:702-707.
Davies, R., Butler, N., and Goldstein, H. (1972) From
    Birth to Seven. London: Longmans.
Ditmore, J., Jr., and Prosser, W. R. (1973) A Study
    of Day Care's Effects on the Labor Force
    Participation of Low-Income Mothers. Washington,
    D.C.: Office of Economic Opportunity.

Doyle, A., and Somers, K. (1975) The Effects of Group and Family Day Care on Infant Attachment. Paper presented at the meeting of the Canadian Psychological Association, Quebec, June 1975.

Eliot, M. (1962) The Children's Bureau: fifty years of public responsibility for action on behalf of children. American Journal of Public Health 52(4):576-577.

Etaugh, C. (1980) Effects of nonmaternal care on children: research evidence and popular views. American Psychologist 35:309-319.

Fein, G. (1976) Infant Day Care and the Family: Regulatory Strategies to Ensure Parent Participation. Mimeographed report prepared for the Assistant Secretary for Planning and Evaluation, U.S. Department of Health, Education, and Welfare.

Fogelman, K. (1976) Research feedback: Britain's sixteen-year-olds. In Concern. Volume 21. London: National Children's Bureau.

Golden, M., Rosenbluth, L., Grossi, M., Policare, H., Freeman, H., and Brownlee, E. (1978) The New York City Infant Day Care Study. New York: Medical and Health Research Association of New York City.

Haring, B. (1976) Special Report on Funding of CWLA Voluntary Agency Members: 1960-1975. New York: Child Welfare League of America.

Hayes, C., and Davis, C. (1979) Early childhood: the content and management of social research and development in selected federal agencies. In Laurence E. Lynn, Jr., Studies in the Management of Social Research and Development: Selected Policy Areas. Study Project on Social Research and Development, National Research Council. Washington, D.C.: National Academy of Sciences.

Hill, J. (1973) Some Perspectives on Adolescence in American Society. Unpublished paper commissioned by the Office of Child Development, U.S. Department of Health, Education, and Welfare.

Joint Commission on Mental Health of Children (1970) Crisis in Child Mental Health: Challenge for the 1970's. New York: Harper and Row.

Kagan, J. (1976) The Effect of Day Care on the Infant. Mimeographed report prepared for the Assistant Secretary for Planning and Evaluation, U.S. Department of Health, Education, and Welfare.

Kamerman, S. (1980) Parenting in an Unresponsive Society: Managing Work and Family. New York: Free Press.

Kamerman, S., and Kahn, A. (1981) Childcare, Family Benefits, and Working Parents. New York: Columbia University Press.

Kenniston, K., and the Carnegie Council on Children (1978) All Our Children. New York: Harcourt, Brace, Jovanovich.

Kirst, M., Garms, W., and Opperman, T. (1980) State services for children: an exploration of who benefits, who governs. Public Policy 28(2):190-191.

Lynn, L. E., Jr. (1978) Fiscal and Organizational Constraints on Family Policy. Harvard University Discussion Paper Series. #55D. April.

National Research Council (1976) Toward a National Policy for Children and Families. Advisory Committee on Child Development. Washington, D.C.: National Academy of Sciences.

National Research Council (1978) The Federal Investment in Knowledge of Social Problems. Report of the Study Project on Social Research and Development. Washington, D.C.: National Academy of Sciences.

New York State Association for Retarded Children v. Carey, U.S. District Court, New York, 1975, 393 F. Supp. 715 (E.D. NY 1975).

Panel on Youth of the President's Science Advisory Committee (1974) Youth: Transition to Adulthood. Chicago: University of Chicago Press.

Powell, D. (1977a) Day Care and the Family: A Study of Interactions and Congruency. Detroit: Merrill-Palmer Institute.

Powell, D. (1977b) The Interface Between Families and Child Care Programs: A Study of Parent-Caregiver Relationships. Detroit: Merrill-Palmer Institute.

Powell, D. (1978a) The interpersonal relationship between parents and caregivers in day care settings. *American Journal of Orthopsychiatry* 48:680-689.

Powell, D. (1979) Toward a socio-ecological perspective of relations between parents and child care programs. In S. Kilmer, ed., *Advances in Early Education and Day Care*. Vol. I. Greenwich, Conn.: JAI Press.

Prescott, E.A. (1973) Comparison of Three Types of Day Care and Nursery School/Home Care. Paper presented at the meeting of the Society for Research in Child Development, Philadelphia, March 1973.

Rapoport, R., and Rapoport, R. (1977) *Fathers, Mothers, and Society*. New York: Basic Books.

Riccinti, H. (1976) Effects of Infant Day Care Experience on Behavior and Development: Research and Implications for Social Policy. Mimeographed report prepared for the Assistant Secretary for Planning and Evaluation, U.S. Department of Health, Education, and Welfare.

Rivlin, A. (1972) Child care. In C. L. Schultze et al., eds., *Setting National Priorities: The 1973 Budget*. Washington, D.C.: Brookings Institution.

Robinson, H., and Robinson, N., eds. (1972-1979) *International Monograph Series on Early Child Care*. London: Gordon and Breach.

Robinson, H., Robinson, N., Wolius, M., Bronfenbrenner, U., and Richmond, J. (1973) *Early Child Care in the United States of America*. New York: Gordon and Breach.

Rose, R. (1976) Government programs affecting children: the federal budget, FY 1974-1976. Part of *A Study of Research and Development Needs for the Making of Social Policy Toward Young Children*. Volume VII. Unpublished paper prepared for the National Science Foundation.

Ruopp, R., Travers, J., Cohen, C., and Glautz, F. (1979) *Children at the Center: Final Report of the National Day Care Study*. Volume I. Cambridge, Mass.: Abt Books.

Shaw, C. R., et al. (1929) *Delinquency Areas: A Study of the Geographic Distribution of School Truants, Juvenile Delinquents, and Adult Offenders in*

99

Chicago. Behavior Research Monographs. Chicago: University of Chicago Press.

Sheehan, D. (1977) The Children's Puzzle: A Study of Services to Children in Massachuetts. Boston, Mass.: Institute for Governmental Services.

Shyne, A., and Schroeder, A. (1978) National Study of Social Services to Children and Their Families. Washington, D.C.: U.S. Government Printing Office.

Sjlund, A. (1973) Day Care Institutions and Children's Development. Lexington, Mass.: D.C. Heath.

Spergel, I. (1964) Racketville, Swontown, Haulgerg: An Exploratory Study of Delinquency Subcultures. Chicago: University of Chicago Press.

Steiner, G. (1971) The State of Welfare. Washington, D.C.: Brookings Institution.

Steiner, G. (1976) The Children's Cause. Washington, D.C.: Brookings Institution.

Strasburg, P. (1978) Violent Delinquents: A Report to the Ford Foundation from the Vera Institute. New York: Monarch.

UNCO, Inc. (1975) National Day Care Consumer Study. Prepared for the Office of Child Development, U.S. Department of Health, Education, and Welfare.

U.S. Department of Labor (1980) Perspectives on Working Women: A Databook. Bureau of Labor Statistics Bulletin 2080. Washington, D.C.: U.S. Government Printing Office.

U.S. Office of Management and Budget (1977) Special Analyses, Budget of the U.S. Government. Washington, D.C.: U.S. Government Printing Office.

Werner, E. (1979) Cross Cultural Child Development. Monterey, Calif.: Brooks/Cole Publishing Company.

Wiltse, K. (1978) Current issues and new directions in foster care. In Child Welfare Strategy in the Coming Years. Washington, D.C.: Office of Human Development Services, U.S. Department of Health, Education, and Welfare.

Wyatt v. Stickney, U.S. District Court, Alabama, 1971, 325 F. Supp. 871.